the joy and terror
are both in the swallowing

christine shan shan hou

After Hours Editions
New York ◆ Kingston
afterhourseditions.com

Cover design by Eric Amling
Typesetting by Adam Robinson
Editors: Sarah Jean Grimm & Eric Amling

Library of Congress Control Number: 2020948709

First edition
ISBN: 978-1-7334082-3-3

FSC® Certified

MIX
Paper from
responsible sources
FSC® C011935

FOR SENNA AND PIA

CONTENTS

THE LOST HAIKUS

/ / /

THE LOST HAIKUS

/ / /

AMANUENSIS

(AFTER FRANÇOISE GILOT)

I imagine killing all the ants in my apartment with my smallest vibrator
I make them dance and shake, give them little seizures
Like my body when I come.
Submission is easiest when done alone.
I identify more with a doormat than a goddess.
A misfit cumulus cloud reaches its fingers upward
Towards a larger network of clouds
In hopes of landing a new job in the cloudy marketplace.
Networking is what you make of it.
You can be the woman who says yes or the woman who says no.
I don't expect to see leopard prints on young women
But when I do I make a run for it.
The survival rate is higher for those who don't react in ugly situations
But I am not afraid of death or the little bruises I pick up along the way.
I can get down naked on all fours and be the woman who says yes
Even though I am the woman who says no.

PEREGRINATION

The woman tried to bite her tongue off
A Chinese form of committing suicide

Watch the entire night disappear unto itself
A murdering den with golden arrows

Famous for its fragility
Lack of fertility, fabulous mobility

One must sever a leg in order
To understand their impulses

A tongue is not a limb
But an escape route

Into the arena of tiny decisions
Where an opportunity

Presents itself in the form of a five-pointed star
Lone pawn overlooking pond of crooked pawns

Everything that happens within a lifetime becomes
Less new by the hour

Luminous spheres roll out of celestial bodies
Little errands on the run

Those found dragging their feet
Will be picked up one-by-one

& taken to a third place
A neck of land surrounded by water

Where small children grow into ugly children
& vanish through windows in the middle of the night

BLUE DESERT

One person believes in torture
While another person does not

A believer always wins
A non-believer does not

Every day piles of pebbles are being tortured beneath the sun
Every day a desert remains intact

Every day you do the best for your health
You do your best to keep your body alive

Pounding is a part of it
Feelings of irrelevance are at the heart of it

You go searching for a flirtatious encounter
When the smog clears, instant arousal

Love is two-fold, but it could also be more
You want more, but that is a luxury

You want so badly that you cannot fall asleep
You drink a sleeping potion to help you sleep

You dream you are in a town with blue hills
You eat at a foreign restaurant

You are wearing a blue dress patterned with daisies
In the dream you are a little girl

You have no choice but to act like a little girl
You are eating a peach

You are holding tightly onto a string that is tied to the sun
You let go of the string and feel separation anxiety

Then you wake up alone in a room
You are one pebble in a pile of pebbles

You imagine yourself as a boulder
And bask in the afternoon sun

NO RAIN NO RAIN

FOR FRANKIE CHABRIER

Frankie said that giving birth
is a pain that feels both ancient
and modern.
Some people are incapable
of communicating their love
when everything is clouded by grief.
Short-term goals include:
Buy new clothes one size up
and laugh more and often.
Not knowing how much pain
is involved in an act can make you
see things that aren't even there.
Freedom can end up looking a lot
like abandonment, especially if you
are a caterpillar.
Going into labor marks the beginning
of a separation as well as the dawn of
a new regime.
No rain, no rain
she said while waving her
hand over the giant machine.
Rain makes way for rot
and you don't have the right
to rot away.

NEW AGE EXPEDITION

You love to call out the bad guys then leave
the scenario unblemished.
Characters are known to wander
in the cinema of the psyche.
A full on terrace is constructed at the peak of it.
A terrace of the mind is optimal in a new age of development,
Empirical data insists on offering something
that wasn't even theirs to begin with.
You can always explore other options.
You can always opt out of the meal plan.
You can always stop at any point in time
and demand something bigger.
Ancient diseases are stored in
ice as big as a mountain.
You have to work hard to unlearn the facts.
History happens all at once in a string of inconveniences.
The instinct is to resort to brutality.
The instinct is to throw everything into a moat full of crocodiles.
The moat surrounds an oracle the size of a house.
Moths circle the oracle.
Contemplate the concept of deep time
Time and no time are the same thing.
All of this thinking interferes with this evening's plans.
Maybe don't have kids.
Believe whole-heartedly in the journey.
Take over the amazon.
Treat everything like a blank canvas and
write your name all over it.
Hang it in your terrace for all your guests to see.
Sleep with each guest and then pretend like it didn't happen.
You can spend a lifetime asleep and still know that more dying
is coming.
You can spend a lifetime studying a single planet religiously.
You keep a book of numbers on your bedside table.

It is made of cardboard like your fantasies.
In order for the new age parable to work,
someone has to survive it.
You are not used to being provoked like this.
The instinct is to resort to brutality.
Let the moths take care of it.

The Lost Haikus

SKY

Little girl riding
flying goose, geography
is obedient

CLEANSE

Interior mouth
kingdom, accumulation
tastes of lemon trees

GLAZED APPARATUS

Replace the missing
object—slathered in honey—
complete without you

TO DO

Make toast for a tree
Sleep one thousand years, delay
gratification

BATH

The internet is
a place to live your fiction
in a heart-shaped tub

POND

Sitting lotus twins
alone in pond, glass-eyed
reluctant, tender

SOFT PORNOGRAPHY

A woman rides a man
    for 45-minutes on a loop

on a small CRT TV
    in a small room

for medical purposes
    fake injections

        work better
        than fake pills

        but fake surgeries
are the most powerful

        A warm pill
evaporates a soul

        dictates the arrangement
        of particles

inside an apple
    fed to the woman

with too much pressure
        on her head

        The dirt
        makes life more doomy

        an end is both near
        & far

        A daughter

who wants dramatic
visual effects

marries a man who eats
40,000 tons of food
in one day

then shatters a bridge
with his teeth

What looks like peaks
of a marriage

are hard clouds   in formation
according to the
cloud appreciation society

Not all clouds have meanings
behind them

not all visions
are pure

Like looking up at the sky
but seeing the sea
roiling

What is the secret
to popularity

in a chorus
of saints?

What appears striking
from a distance

                        is a lazy
                    stinking animal
            marching towards the scent
                                    of distant rain

                    whose own scent rapidly
                        delivers change

        in a smooth era   what a smooth &
                                     violent era

AWAKENING YOURSELF

It was all merry-making at first
God works on a needlepoint

Of a landscape of a mountain
Its peak in the clouds

Thinking

Sleeping king on a hill
Head encased in mysterious mist

God wears a pink garb
With another white cloth
Draped over his heavy shoulders

I wonder if needlepointing is what
Keeps one well-rounded

If an airplane falls from the sky
Who will catch it?

Today is today
Tomorrow is an arrangement
Of something blossomy & coniferous

The sea is a leathery chair
The highway is the living room

Let this poem be a game
of radical endurance

Whoever wakes up first
is the winner

BAYOU

A tiny turtle with two heads crawls out of a glass box
A skull-shaped cloud looms over something big and blue

I am a perfectionist and not sensible in the least
I spy on my neighbors and pet their pets
I shoot a cloud in the sky to expose the universal forms
of a mother and child

These forms radiate outward into planetary orbs,
tendrils, and vertebrae-like networks.

There are lives that are built entirely around going to the doctor
There are lives that are built entirely on the delay of gratification
There are paintings that come to life with the goal
of becoming three-dimensional

How greedy of me to want to live a simple country life with shy people

Out in the bayou
I travel at breakneck speeds
through lukewarm waters

THE JOY AND TERROR ARE
BOTH IN THE SWALLOWING

May my daughter never resemble a sullen cabbage.
Running jostles the organs within the rickety confines

of a torso, like rearranging your body's furniture to give view
to a swimming pool. The swimming pool possesses the same

qualities as other swimming pools. It is blue and vague.
How suddenly a thought can unglue you and make you fall

into pieces. Each piece, a new country captivated by southern light.
In the south, spirits follow false passageways.

Bright young people mark their territory by repeating simple
tasks in an invigorating manner.

Bright young people need adventure, a heated portable incubator for
processed foods and aspirations governed in by new technologies.

A rigid awareness dawns over the heart smothering my whole purpose
in life and arousing my womanly insecurity around machinery.

It's good to do the work even if you want to do horrible
things with the results. Cataloging the day's sugar intake is one form

of reason if you have gestational diabetes.
My daughter doesn't know what she wants unless I show it to her.

I said: You cannot rely on algorithms to take you to your destination.
I said: There are ways to be wanted that have yet to be discovered.

SUNDAY AFTERNOON

The day spreads out its limbs
in order to know what it truly wants

I stare into a lightbox
to study pure happiness

An opal atop my palm reluctantly
turns into a grape

All lost limbs come from the same lonely place
where the terror of the day meets

The terror of the night
The afternoon relaxes its tired shoulders

Onto feathers
& dark matter

This is a fable about the lengths to which
I will go to become my most enlightened self

I hang upside down obediently like a
little brown bat

FABLE

There was a neighborhood
that was scared of bears
They hid their children in
cars and closets
guarded them with brooms
and knives
One man who knew no such fear
befriended the bears
At lunchtime the bears
would gather around and
eat out of his hands
After dinner they would
sleep next to him
in sleeping sacks
The thing is
Not everyone is afraid to die
or wear the same outfit twice
I wear an old brown
bathing suit on Monday, Tuesday,
and Wednesday.
The elastic in the straps
makes a snapping sound
as I tie it around my neck
and watch my neighbors
move their cars back
and forth
I see them at the store
buying varieties of milk
I catch them looking at
their reflections in
storefront windows
gleaming
I spy on them at night
from behind dazzling blue curtains

LIKE IT NEVER HAPPENED

A sculpture miraculously appears in the rafters.

An obtrusive tchotchke indicating the presence of unholy forces.

Imagine holding a miniature version of yourself tightly.

Having good intentions vs. bad intentions does not keep religious beliefs alive.

Little acrobats line up in the streets in preparation for doomsday.

Floral and vegetal forms from heaven fly over the landscape.

It is natural to be scared when teetering on the precipice of change.

It is natural to keep your refrigerator stocked with frozen dinners:

Hot dogs, macaroni, turkey, peas, and mashed potatoes.

Cindy says that she loves things that are magically clear.

Clarity is a moment of madness unravelling in real time in a public space.

We are all members of the public with dreadful hometowns and pathetic hearts.

We tell ourselves: Fake can be just as good! Then slink back into our pattern-seeking ways.

While contemplating whether or not to eat a clay pot, small anonymous faces appear in low reliefs around the pot's surface.

I eat it after reading somewhere that consuming clay has major health benefits.

Recent history shows that the preservation of authenticity is a hoax and that everything is subject to change.

There are days I am so enthralled with habit that I truly cannot be bothered.

Everything is subject to turn into glass.

The warm bodies of my friends emanate golden lines like the sun.

I am wide awake.

How magnificently clear is the day.

BRIDAL SHOWER

Time is an antiquated baking mold
& I am the cake batter
Driveling
in a loosey-goosey manner
A vulnerability that can be recognized
& reshaped
I want to keep my private parts private
protected from rain
& contained within their own
elaborate system
A gravitational force
pulling away
from stars
star pilgrims & star bears
The future feeling bleak & sudden
like purchasing a house
or a lifestyle
atop a cloud
where an oracle
sits and scribbles in a notebook
Time to get a spine!
Time to forcibly separate the males from the females
Time to leave bisexual ways behind
& pull the mind-body lever
There's always someone who makes you be feminine
There's always a guest who makes you feel irrelevant
over the holiday weekend
The idea of bonus fills me with joy
Jules who wears red, white, and blue
Suggests hypnosis as a way of unlearning
the things that I knew
Of course sudden brushes with fame
do not lead to a happy ending
In fact I know that fame will be

the primary source of our destruction
I know the uncomfortable facts of natural flavors
& how they inevitably disrupt the body's flora
Let's learn how to say thank you
without the calories
Let's divide the gardens between
those who do not know they are dead
& those who do
Two faint symbols blinking out from a plotless void
Let's agree to live in a social compact
Sometimes we are going to hurt each other

SOME FACTS ABOUT MYSELF

After the physical therapist said that the pain is mostly in my head,
my arm has been hurting less.

That is the power men have on my psyche.

I learned how to throw a cocktail party for strangers from
my mother and my grandmother.

At night I grind lifesavers with my teeth and then spit them out into
the sky.

Scrape up the mess of stars and black stuff and place it in a vial for
analysis.

Blue mouthguard paired with blue roll of tape on bedside table

The color blue is a stand-in for me and all the options I could be at this
exact moment in time.

Secretly, I just wanted to hear Jules say the word *crudités*.

I wish I were an alternative singer-songwriter that could carry a tune.

I wish I knew how to fall in love with a doctor.

My favorite type of man is a Midwestern dreamboat with a five o'clock
shadow.

My favorite song is a love song written by Swedish people who have
never fallen in love.

NEW TOWN

The man asked if I preferred tigers or elephants.
A tiger is an obvious selection so I say elephant and
quickly walk away. At the market I do not like to be
bothered so I continue to touch every piece of fruit
and examine them for bruises and blemishes. I do not
have a golden touch but if I did, it would quickly turn
the day lackadaisical like stale rain in a bucket.
A new town emerges from the rain and becomes a
bigger version of the modern home. Old neighborhoods
spill into a river making up much of the morning news.
One man caught a fish with his umbrella and then made
soup with the head and tail. Eating becomes a reminder
of livelihood. Everything I touch sinks. I try to think happy
thoughts but am scared of attachment so I think about
blonde movie stars and their fading stardoms. Sometimes
I think about tigers, elephants, and giraffes. Try to guess
how many strands of hair are on my head. Once the juices
have settled I will elaborate.

A LITTLE BIT OF HURT

When a woman humiliates
     a man, everyone
          has to pay
A small group of founders
          spread diseases amongst
               themselves,
I've never seen anything like it
     I am a simple farmer's wife
          that has never felt
          so alive
Yet so out of sorts
Some people can't even handle
               chicken stock
This is where society is split
          down the middle
It's like you have all of the time
in the world
          but you don't
It is easy to recognize one voice
     as familiar and one
               as an intruder
A space anomaly can throw
     the solar system off balance
An educational video game makes
     earth's surroundings
          even more real
A big galaxy gobbles a tiny one
          and I place a penny on
               my husband's forehead
What happens to the massive
     amounts of information
          is unknown
But most likely pulled into singularity
               cramming

all of my hopes and
dreams into
a pea-sized hole
Are the biggest holes the result of two holes forming
or one hole eating a lot?
The answer to this question is
what you need
to get the job done
My other television feels meaningless

SEVEN WONDERS

I would like to be friendly with everyone on the planet
including the megafauna.

I bank on other people's forgiveness so I don't have
to do the work of change.

I bank on nature's forgiveness too.
I leave enormous tips to show off my wealth

and gratitude for the service industry.
Speaking of services, I love my stationary bike

because it can transport me to any of the Seven Wonders
without having to stay in a traditional hotel.

The afterlife is the same as real life except
everyone lives in a hotel.

In my real life, my husband works for a hotel
that is slowly falling apart due to family differences.

The truth is: some people can't stand to see other people
having fun in their summer bodies and paper gowns.

For my last day on this planet I'd like to write about
the peculiar light that shines through my bedroom window.

Here is a picture of me in my bed without makeup on.
Don't I look stunning?

I am bland in my lack of curvature
Content as an apple, fragrant as an onion

LOVE STORY

Upper hands feast on the marmalade of the dead

An act of God followed by a blind but kind feeling

An enormous hand sweeping its wrinkly fingers over the earth

Loose marbles all rolling towards the same inevitability

I would do anything to give birth to a saint

To learn how to end the process of deliberation without breaking my spirit

Buildings undulate in a once-flat city

What starts as a pragmatic relationship between two men quickly turns into primitive love impulse

Neighbors aimlessly walk around a village built over a wide network of lakes

A decision made based on convenience proves to be a terrible idea

A god on a Corinthian column planted in the center of a city overlooks a sea of traffic

I gaze up at it and think of something rare like the last sexual experience in the world and whether there are circumstances where betrayal is allowed

The hardest part of self-practice is keeping your eyes open

The hardest part of keeping your eyes open is having to take responsibility for the reckoning

A reckless teenager is swallowed up by a crack that splits open in the middle of a sidewalk

Winnicott says: *When it comes to having our lives planned out for us, heaven help us if the thinkers take over!*

A woman without a plan hides on a roof at night and gives birth to a girl and a pig

I transmit a tiny bolt of electricity into the pig's head

Sending shockwaves into a city where women hold up half the sky

On the main highway, Jesus offers each driver a new life in the form of a monarch butterfly

I know that the ones with the upper hand are the ones with the story

Upper hands determine what kind of fear is credible and what kind is not

Upper hands live in comfortable homes by the seaside

Upper hands resist change so intensely that the rest of their body has no choice but to disintegrate

I wonder what it feels like to be magically torn apart in a surprising display that burns down 45,000 acres of farmland

A wildfire makes gender all the more insignificant

Gender being nothing but an iteration of sentimentality and shame

I want to die the most beautiful death in the deepest blue sea

I want my death to be comfortable and homey, but also victorious and sexy like a pack of half-naked men riding wild animals

A fleet of monarch butterflies descends from a tall shaft of sunlight into a sea of traffic

A love story in the distance fans out its feathery wings

There was a time I was much braver than I am now

There was a time I accidentally flowered through my pants, breaking the zipper

My distant cousins glowing the entire time

What first was a shack in the center of the city becomes a birthing center for saints

Accused of a crime

Forced into a confession

Forced into their true nature: A dangling piece of fruit estranged from its tree

Treeless tundra with a barely visible horizon and no landmarks

A birthmark from the heavens received with open hands and open faces

ON FRIDAYS THEY GO DANCING

dead women arrive
   on demand along a highway
   south of Los Angeles

where factory workers
     pull from the interior of
  a city   a less identifiable form

    say a crystal
    that gets rubbed
   around the eyes

   for the purpose of
    expanding peripheral vision
   by one hundred percent

   dropping hard candy
    into a birdbath
that has accumulated water

   over the years
losing all its flavor & purpose
   a reminder

to think things through
    their most extreme
     consequences

   knowing that the responsibility
   of your body is
    yours & yours

    alone & the desire
   to be handsome while wearing

a three-piece suit

outweighs grievances carried
    over   in a silver suitcase
        from past lives

a voyage into another timeline
    reveals a laissez-faire
    system of points

            where collective madness
    makes itself felt
        in killings

inside the factories
    that run   along the highway
        south of Los Angeles

The Lost Haikus

WESTERN THOUGHT

Inside a suburb
the eyes of numerous see
unspeakable things

PELVIS

Between your legs a
fruit bowl suggests the future
uninhabited

RURAL PLEASURES

Thin green ribbons tied
around gnarled tree trunks, young tongues
licking village winds

LEFTOVERS

Sorrow lingers—
opposite of the fish that
rots from the head down

SAFE

A prison is a
prison and the beginning
of my love for you

PAUSE

Inside a city
there will always be spaces
to breathe in between

DEVIATION

Crimson moon behind
pernicious cloud, submission
is never a sin

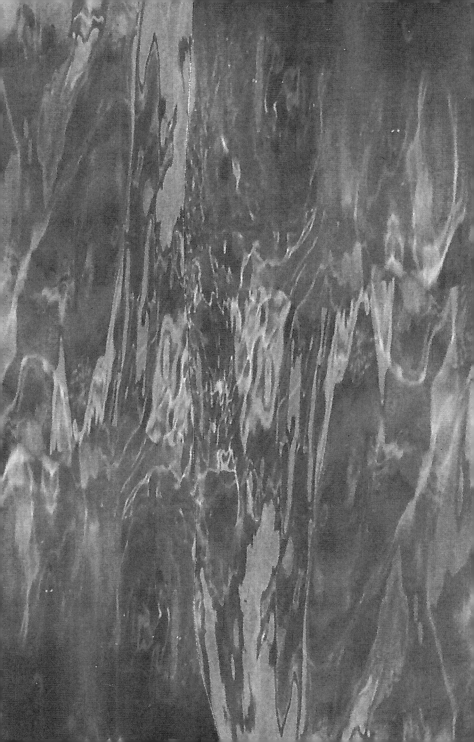

AFTERLIFE

When one predator is matched with one thousand prey
they do not recognize it as a threat

Learned helplessness means clinging on to superstition
like gripping a metal bar with your teeth

You cannot self-acceptance your way out of it
You cannot use technology to get away from other technology

Fear is the consequence of being
There is momentum to fear

Just like there is momentum to women
rid of their medicinal uses

Safety in numbers cannot be your only defense
You solve a puzzle

The puzzle comes to life
and is repulsed by your fear of death

You make it entertainment
You know exactly where you are going

You have no idea where you are going
You are tethered to a maypole in a meadow of poppies

You clamor for permission to feel
a distinctly western feel

a large leftover
a morning commute

a thigh
a breast

NOT A NEW THEORY OF EVOLUTION

> A repository is crammed with stuffed monkeys and ivory carvings, snow leopard coats and dried seal penises, chairs with tails and lamps with hooves.
>
> – Rachel Nuwer, "A Mausoleum for Endangered Species"

The natural process of selection shows that those desperate
to appear easygoing never were.

Making one uninformed decision can leave you dead.
Protection is not so much a right as ideology dictated
by a tall figure at the head of the table.

When feeding into a new sentiment, there is no accounting for taste.
The human appetite for other species cannot be satiated.

You can either devote your resources to reversing past wrongs
or prevent new ones from happening.

You can choose to feel shame for the materials that you own
and the women you leave in the past.

There is something spiritual about your vanity and laziness
that is thrilling to witness.

Choose dutifully, horse.
You who are made of hunger and prey.

PIECE OF EVIDENCE

a visitor
a settler

a guest
a purveyor

a gift
a psychology

a drawer
for confidential matter

a hand
at striking distance

a frontispiece
an induction

deliberately sloppy
transition

a transgression
a refusal of the future

an important algorithm
an unexpected euphemism

a refusal of the past
an unforeseeable circumstance

a heart grown from plastic
maybe beginning

a family matter
a load of laundry

a habit nurtured into fruition
a health reason

a fruit bowl
but with onions

a refusal
a refusal

a chance
a resignation

a clamoring
for permission

for entertainment
a consideration of the facts

a more modern approach
a dispersion

a monthly allowance
a solution

a reversal of direction
a roll of fat

a bread roll for later
a discarded piece of furniture

a reinterpretation of a certain age
an urgent affair

a systematic deflection
of the problem

a dewdrop
for succulence

a reversal of a herd
a hurdle

DISTANT RELATIVE

It's OK to sing without knowing the words.

An outsider becomes an insider
and then disappears with the megafauna.

It won't be long until I become the last of my kind
and shrivel into the bushes.

Tread lightly, do not let sentiment go to waste.

A new fossil is discovered to be
a distant relative of a horse.

A rare, medicinal plant produces an unusual smell, winds
carry the scent from one continent to another.

What will it take to convince you that I am a woman of science?

Tread lightly.

How easy it is to become the worst of both worlds.

This is for those whose songs we will not know.

THE DANGER SEEKERS

An outsider spoils
the whole show with his naive
understanding of
primitivism

Sometimes you have to hide inside a precious egg
other times it makes more sense just to live in
the jungle

The problem with planning ahead of time is not knowing
when to stop
like a gymnast
in the middle
of a floor routine

Depending on today's gender some loungewear is restrictive
while other garments give more meaning
to the day

In India
families send scantily-dressed elders out
into dangerous areas
to gamble with tigers

Nameless forces twist
this way & that
pushing the day
towards its fateful climax

In the case of death outside the reservation
you may receive a token of appreciation
a payout
a bouquet of hibiscus
a reassuring phone call
a golden arrow
a pressed dollar bill

NEVER CURSED

The surgeon couldn't cut it out
Because how can you cut out bone without
disturbing the entire infrastructure
A handsaw is an ideal tool used for removal
as are tweezers
You can tweeze the hairs out
of your nose and around your genitals
You can tweeze the ants from off the kitchen floor
Consider this text as the beginning
of an arduous goodbye process
Coming together as a family for one last soirée
I even take the time to wash my legs with soap
Last night I was having a hard time falling asleep
Because of my noisy air conditioner
So I took a Xanax
Taking Xanax is like going to Canada
Idyllic, soothing, at times rapturous
When I think about my trips to Canada
I think about all the surgeries that I have
undergone to get me to where I am today
When I am in the operating room my job is to
hold the halo as still as possible
just like this

SENNA LOVES HER CAR SEAT MORE THAN SHE LOVES THE TREES

I want to live a country life
in this big city

I want to want
to have sex again

To feel my organs labor inside
their cardboard boxes

I wander aimlessly down
the aisles of a department store

In hopes of discovering a magic formula
to keeping myself young and attractive

Tiny organs strapped into car seats
await travel to fantastical places

Cars in friendly neighborhoods drive
around in circles until they fall apart

I fall in love with a blouse on sale
the color of a forest

Where wings that once were elbows
hang guilelessly from trees

The Lost Haikus

SAD

Autumn leaves stagger
amongst midnight, weeping trees
sleep unevenly

AFTERHOURS

Learned helplessness from
family and friends, tiny screens
divine long faces

VIEW

Wind turbine stirring
sky, lone creature in disguise
lazy flying bird

BABY GEOMETRY

Flat bottomless tree
swallows everything in sight
Indigestibles!

PREMONITION

Pink saint harbinger
Ornamental galaxies
Devour dynasties

HARVEST

The onion detects
certainty in dirt, on
the contrary, shame

VISITOR EXPERIENCE

Interior with
venetian red, unable
to move—death comes fast

KIND OF BLUE

(AFTER MATTHEW WONG)

Moon leashed to wood post
Blue still life trembles while stares
Haunted, coughing boy

PLAYGROUND

When I am tired
I lay my head down in a tunnel to rest
It is not possible to live your best
Life in a tunnel
Even if there are holes punctured
Along the sides of it
Holes designed for children
to look out into the world
A way of compartmentalizing
abstract thoughts
That are small enough to fit
In the palm of my hand
What is the difference between a trowel
and this here, toy trowel?
What does it mean to be more adult-like?
Digging into our beliefs can help us stay
committed to our morals when the fight
gets bleak
When my daughter grows tired she lays
her head down in a tunnel to rest
She is so small that she could stand upright
inside of it
While for me
it is just another crawlspace
The difference between me and my daughter
is size and money
and hormones
Giving money away because it feels good
can be described as philanthropy
I could purchase this land
with my two hands any day of the week

TRUST EXERCISE

When I visit
my esthetician

I lay on my back
& open my body

into a diamond
Peel off a layer

of my face
& soften my head

into the table
Even though

I am inside
a synthetic forest

I pretend I am
in an office cubicle

Directly beneath
the sun

The cubicle sits
atop a pyramid

which sits atop a lake
Everyday my fingers

grow longer & my eyes
grow wide like shapeless lakes

Everyday my love gets
firmer & drier

& the slightest bit fishier
Like bonito flakes

drifting away from
the center of the bowl

& towards the light
Everything moves in

opposition to death
My fingers move with pleasure

into your mouth
Instant transformation

is possible when
terrifying your offspring

into submission
Thank God

I live in this day & age
where the women

are heavenly & bountiful
Thank God

I can do a cartwheel
Thank God

For natural lighting
For lightening the mood

HEAVEN

I walk, facing forward for the first time
And see green

There is a mystery to be solved
An epiphany

A bunch of flowers
A classic chubby stick

A kidney-shaped pool
A shape that is the combination of all of those things

A shiny stone bench overseeing a small pond
An overgrowth of lily pads

What you wear can lead to your next best friend or your new career
This is called reward-based mentality

What a discovery
To experience pain and not know why

To feel incomplete
In a land of abundance and milk

Spit milk into a wound
Then split the wound into two

One boy plus one girl
An acute awareness of death may have a stronghold on future
        narratives

I will continue to walk through life in a forward-facing manner
Towards water and hills

Towards fruit-bearing trees and temples
Towards bougainvilleas

I will feel heavy with belief and loyalty
& look a certain way on the outside

While feeling an uncertain way on the inside
I will carry a bouquet of bougainvilleas to my next significant
        life event

I sit on a pile of sticks and count my eyelashes
Each eyelash worth its weight in gold

The day is nearing its end
The window curtains painted gold and black

I mourn the loss of small worlds while observing roaring rivers
I wonder what it feels like to be elderly

I am disappointed in the parts of my body that ache
I succumb to a fugue state

I have no common sense
& worship a single thought for no good reason

In heaven I am hot to the touch
It will be a miracle that I survive

SECOND PARADISE

Tame animals majestically return into the wild
The pageantry unfolding in the
Slowest of motions

Every donkey, ox, horse & sheep
Running away into the wilderness
Completely forgetting their previous nature

A second paradise
Opaque & without backstory
Flora breathe into the faces of elders

Smashed against rocks
This is what is called
The female pleasure gap

It is real & gaping
& smells of the greenest grasses
Where long limbs grow towards heaven

To honor the judges they love
& the judges they don't

ENDNOTES

In the poem, "New Age Expedition" the line: "time and no time are the same thing" is by Arda Collins from: "Dusk: An Interview with Arda Collins" in Bomb Magazine from January 25, 2012.

"Awakening Yourself" was written in response to Yorgos Lathimos' *Dogtooth* (2009).

"Bayou" was written in response to Andrei Konchalovsky's *Shy People* (1987). The italicized line is by Emily Cheng from the interview series *Beer with a Painter: Emily Cheng* conducted by Jennifer Samet in Hyperallergic Weekend from July 8, 2017. HTTPS://HYPERALLERGIC.COM/389340/BEER-WITH-A-PAINTER-EMILY-CHENG/

"The Joy and Terror are Both in the Swallowing" is a line from Diane Arbus as quoted in *Diane Arbus: Portrait of a Photographer* by Arthur Lubow, (Ecco 2016), p. 183

In "Bridal Shower," the line: "There's always someone who makes you be feminine" is from Alice Notley's *Certain Magical Acts*, p.55. And: "Two faint symbols blinking / out from a plotless void" is from Jia Tolentino's essay "The Improbably Insanity of CATS" published in *The New Yorker* on December 16, 2019.

In "A Little Bit of Hurt," the line: "Are the biggest holes the result of two holes forming / or one hole eating a lot?" is from "An Earthling's Guide to Black Holes" by Joanna Klein published in *The New York Times* on June 8, 2016: HTTPS://WWW.NYTIMES.COM/INTERACTIVE/2015/06/08/SCIENCE/SPACE/GUIDE-TO-BLACK-HOLES.HTML

In "Love Story," the line: "Treeless tundra with a barely visible horizon and no landmarks" is from a text message from Niina Pollari.

"On Fridays They Go Dancing" was written in response to Sam Quinones's essay, "The Dead Women of Juárez" in *True Tales from Another Mexico: The Lynch Mob, the Popsicle Kings, Chalino, and the Bronx* (University of New Mexico Press 2001).

"Pause" was written in response to Ursula Eagly's performance, *with gaps for each other,* which premiered at The Chocolate Factory in 2018.

The opening line from "Not a New Theory of Evolution" is from "A Mausoleum for Endangered Species" by Rachel Nuwer published in *The New York Times* on July 10, 2017: HTTPS://WWW.NYTIMES.COM/2017/07/10/SCIENCE/ NATIONAL-WILDLIFE-PROPERTY-REPOSITORY-COLORADO.HTML

"Kind of Blue" was written in response to the paintings of Matthew Wong (1984-2019). The title is borrowed from John Yau's essay, "Matthew Wong: Kind of Blue" published in *Hyperallergic Weekend* on December 17, 2019.

ACKNOWLEDGEMENTS

Earlier versions of many of these poems were published in the following journals:

Ace Hotel Blog; BathHouse Journal; Black Sun Lit; Dreginald; Foundry Journal; La Vague Journal; No, Dear; Poetry Northwest; Powder Keg Magazine; and *The Tiny.* Thank you to all of the editors for providing a first home for these poems.

I am deeply indebted to Cindy Arrieu-King, Niina Pollari, and Frankie Chabrier for their attentiveness, warmth, and friendship. A special thanks to the wonderful Emily Hunt, to whom I owe the thoughtful ordering of the poems in this collection.

I am grateful for my dear friend, Diana Khoi-Nguyen whose 15/15 projects laid the foundation for many of these pieces. You inspire me beyond words.

Thank you to Sarah Jean Grimm and Eric Amling of After Hours Editions for believing in this book and making it a reality. I feel immensely fortunate to work alongside such smart and caring editors.

Lastly, thank you so much to Austin Alter for his love, support, companionship, patience, and tenderness.

Christine Shan Shan Hou is a poet and visual artist. Publications include Community Garden for Lonely Girls (Gramma Poetry 2017), *"I'm Sunlight"* (The Song Cave 2016), *C O N C R E T E   S O U N D* (2011) a collaborative artists' book with Audra Wolowiec, and *Accumulations* (Publication Studio, Jank Editions 2010) featuring drawings by Hannah Rawe. Her poems and artwork have been featured in numerous journals and anthologies.